THE BLESSINGS OF DAILY LIFE

A BALM FOR THE STRESS-FILLED 21ST CENTURY

DEBANJAN ROY

Dedicated to the sacred memory of my Baba (Father), Late Debi Prosad Roy, and Maa (Mother), Late Shubhra Roy.

Now, both of them are not here on this earth in their physical forms.

But I have the strongest faith that they are always with me and guiding me at each and every moment of my life.

So, it is an honour to submit my offering at their lotus feet and seek their blessings.

Contents

Prayers

God is Maa, our Divine Mother.

Maa! Pranam at Your lotus feet!

Maa! Please guide us at all times!

Maa! May we ever walk on Your righteous path in life!

Maa! May we always treasure the jewels you have gifted to each one of us: our parents!

Pranam to Maa!

(Pranam: It is a Sanskrit word that stands for 'Offering Homage')

Acknowledgements

The underlying philosophy of the book is Spirituality.

And, to make this book possible, I am ever grateful to my Guru, Her Holiness, (late) Sri Archana Puri Maa of Sree Satyananda Devayatan, Kolkata.

Her Holiness had graced my life through the sacred 'Mantra Deeksha' (Spiritual Initiation) in 2006. Her blessings have been the continual source of my inspiration ever since I took up the pen and began writing.

Pranam at the lotus feet of my Guru!

Preface

Friends, this book presents a collage of blessings that accrue to us when we pay attention to the nuances of our daily life. Because, as we shall see, when we are observant, then we become alive to how even the most mundane aspect of our day-to-day life can teach us so much.

A simple example will suffice. Most of us are nowadays employed in corporate jobs. We work in offices that are all glitzy, shiny and glass-fronted on the outside. But inside, these offices are filled with a cauldron of negativity: ruthless competition, endless politicking, displays of anger, ever-present tension and so on. The inevitable result of prolonged working in such an environment is the negative vibe, which we then carry to our own homes with imaginable results.

However, while coming out of our offices at the end of any workday, if we simply look up at the evening sky above and thus connect ourselves to Mother Nature for just a few seconds, then something wonderful will happen. First, the ethereal beauty of the red-hued western horizon will elevate our mood. Second and more importantly, the peace of that fleeting sunset hour will silently descend upon us and start cooling our frazzled nerves. And we shall then be able to return to our homes in a much more composed state of mind.

In this manner, we can find the cherished fruits of happiness and peace, nestling in the most routine facet of our daily life. And that is the purpose of writing and sharing this book with you.

With Best Wishes,
Debanjan

A Few Pearls Of Inspiration

Friends, I firmly believe that the wonderful sayings of our great thought leaders are our perennial source of positive thinking. Such wisdom-filled quotes are thus our true jewels.

Therefore, at the start of this book, I would love to share some of my favourite jewels with you:

- I choose to make the rest of my life the best of my life. – Louise Hay
- Man's main task in life is to give birth to himself, to become what he potentially is. – Eric Fromm
- Today is where your book begins, the rest is still unwritten. – Natasha Bedingfield in 'Unwritten'
- And, when you want something, all the universe conspires in helping you achieve it. – Paulo Coelho in 'The Alchemist'
- You have brains in your head. You have feet in your shoes. You can steer yourself in any direction you choose. – Dr Seuss
- Keep your face always towards the sunshine and the shadows will fall behind you. – Walt Whitman
- You don't need to see the whole staircase. Just take the first step. – Martin Luther King Junior
- Blessed is he who has found his work. – Thomas Carlyle
- The man, who is born with the talent which he is meant to use, finds his greatest happiness in using it. - Goethe
- God has made all men to be happy. - Epictetus

Hope the above selection proves to be a source of sustained inspiration for all.

ONE
INTRODUCTION

Friends, the 'Preface' has outlined the objective of this volume. Now, let me share a few thoughts with you on the unique format of this book. You will find that the contents of this narrative are in the form of "Letters": one individual letter is devoted to one specific subject.

These letters got written last over one year as I began observing how, where and on what I'm spending my life. And it was as an observer that I began writing these letters of self-reflection to the humanity at large, whom I regard as my own brothers and sisters. And what I discovered is: our day-to-day life is filled with so many blessings, if we just spend our time more mindfully.

Currently these letters, an outcome of my self-introspection on diverse topics, number over 100. Now, for the purpose of this narrative, I have sought to select 30 of these letters, classify them into separate "Themes" and then present them to you.

These themes are:

- Faith,
- Mother Nature,

- Happiness,
- Goodness,
- Success,
- Attitude,
- Actions and Habits,
- Learning.

In each of these letters, you will find that I have put the crux in the form of bullet points. This is the way I think and write. And I dare say, this makes for easier reading as well.

Hope something within these letters resonates within you and then gradually propels you on the path of self-contemplation yourself, for there lies the key to happiness and peace in our stress-filled lives of the 21st century.

So here we begin...

TWO

The Blessings of Daily Life (Theme: Faith)

Friends, under this sacred theme, I have included the following blessings:

1. God = Good and Good = God
2. Have Daily Conversations with God
3. Righteousness leads to Right Living
4. Serving Man equals Serving God
5. Cleanliness is the Best Way to Move towards Divinity

I am placing these blessings for your kind reading here:

1. God is Good and Good is God

Dear Brothers and Sisters,

Prayers to God for your brilliant success in life. May His protective embrace always keep you and your loved ones enveloped in the warmth of constant joy.

May I now draw your attention to these points please:

- God is the fountain-head of all goodness.
- And all forms of goodness tantamount to worship of God.
- So, whenever we do any good, we are basically offering our homage to God.
- Here the magnitude of our good deed does not matter.
- What truly matters is the goodness of intention in our heart.
- So, let's strive to lead a life of goodness, henceforth.

Wishing you joy as ever,
With love and blessings,
Debanjan

2. Have Daily Conversations with God

Dear Brothers and Sisters,

Prayers to God for your brilliant success in life. May His protective embrace always keep you and your loved ones enveloped in love and abundance.

May I now draw your attention to these points please:

- God is our Divine Father and Mother.
- So, just as we used to tell everything to our parents to clear our heart and mind in our childhood, let us inculcate the same practice in our adulthood also.
- Let us imbibe the golden habit of conversing with God, our Eternal Parent.
- And when we have such daily conversations with God, we can wholeheartedly surrender to Him.

- We can then completely unburden all our sorrows to Him.
- In this manner, we can get restored every day with His Divine compassion.

Wishing you all happiness,
With love and blessings,
Debanjan

3. Righteousness Leads to Right Living

Dear Brothers and Sisters,

Prayers to God for your brilliant success in life. May His protective embrace always keep you and your loved ones enveloped in the warmth of constant joy.

May I now draw your attention to these points please:

- To start with, let us first deeply reflect on the word "Righteousness".
- This profound concept, at its core, stands for uprightness across the entire human spectrum: - spiritual, moral, mental, physical, financial and everything else. Nothing is excluded from its all-inclusive ambit.
- Then we shall come to realise that, it is righteousness that enables us to distinguish right from wrong - it is a manifestation of the fundamental trait of conscience.
- And conscience is something that descends straight from God - it is the one single trait that separates humanity from animality.
- Therefore, when we bring in righteousness into our life, we are basically drawing Divinity into our own life as well.

- In other words, when we are living the righteous life, then our thoughts, speech, actions - everything conforms to the will of God.
- Then such a life blesses us with contentment that is steady - it is not dependent upon anything external - it just bubbles up from deep within, irrespective of the vicissitudes of life and that is the very essence of right living.
- So, tell me, can there be any bigger blessing than the supreme ability to face the ups and downs of life, sheathed in the Godly armour of righteousness?

Wishing you joy as ever,
With love and blessings,
Debanjan

4. Serving man = Serving God

Dear Brothers and Sisters,

Prayers to God for your brilliant success in life. May His protective embrace always keep you and your loved ones enveloped in the warmth of constant joy.

May I now draw your attention to these points please:

- In this post, let's explore the wisdom contained in the captioned idea.
- The credit for articulating this truth afresh in our modern age, goes to Incarnation Supreme, Bhagavan Sri Ramakrishna Dev, when he had uttered the golden formula: "Serve Lord Shiva Himself in the form of living beings".
- And in due course of time, his chief disciple Swami Vivekananda had implemented this stupendous idea in

ground reality, by founding the noble institution of Ramakrishna Mission.

- However, for us lesser mortals, this beautiful percept may not readily strike a chord as we believe that God is in faraway heaven.
- But as Sri Ramakrishna Dev taught us, God is present within each of us.
- Hence, when we start deeply reflecting on this divine saying, we start realising what an extraordinarily significant concept it is, because then our whole creation becomes an extension of God himself.
- With this new understanding, worshipping God acquires a new meaning altogether - we then learn to see God in the homeless beggar on the street - we may choose to feed him with our own hands - it would be such a wonderful homage to God Himself and our own life would get blessed.
- Hence, I request each one of you, to try out this idea for yourself at least once and see the results for yourself.

Wishing you joy at all times,
With love and blessings,
Debanjan

5. Cleanliness = The Best Way towards Divinity in Life

Dear Brothers and Sisters,

Prayers to God for your brilliant success in life. May His protective embrace always keep you and your loved ones enveloped in the warmth of constant joy.

May I now draw your attention to these points please:

- The famous proverb says cleanliness is next to Godliness.
- This golden saying is absolutely true in both letter and spirit.
- Here, cleanliness chiefly stands for the absence of anything, that takes us away from God such as greed, hatred etc.
- By the same token, cultivation of cleanliness paves the road for welcome entry of purity, truthfulness, equanimity and other Godly qualities into our character.
- These divine virtues progressively take us towards the realization of God.
- Thus, when we practice cleanliness of thoughts, we bring in Divinity into our own life.

Wishing you joy as ever,
With love and blessings,
Debanjan

THREE

The Blessings of Daily Life (Theme: Mother Nature)

Friends, under this beautiful theme, I have included the following blessings:

1. Divine Inspiration of Daily Sunrise
2. The Bliss of a Beautiful Flower
3. Rejoice in the dulcet beauty of a Glorious Sunset

I am now placing them for your kind reading here:

1. Divine Inspiration of Daily Sunrise

Dear Brothers and Sisters,

My Prayers to God for a continuous stream of joy, enthusiasm and hope in your life. The same good wishes go to your loved ones as well.

May I now draw your attention to these points please:

1. God is the everlasting source of inspiration.
2. We are all God's children and He sends us His blessings at each step of our life every single day.
3. And the beauty of a sunrise is among the biggest of such blessings.
4. Because through the daily bliss of sunrise, God is telling us –

- "My child! I'm sending you the gift of another brand-new day.
- So, rise.
- Shrug off all of your past disappointments.
- Forget the past.
- A new dawn is here just for you.
- Go out and shine.
- I'm always there with you."

5. Let us therefore always be grateful for this daily blessing of God. And seek His grace to feel inspired as we lead this transient life. And to conclude, my Prayers: God, please bless all your children. And guide them on the right path.

Wishing you all success.

With love and blessings,

Debanjan

2. The Bliss of Beautiful Flower

Dear Brothers and Sisters,

Prayers to God for your brilliant success in life. May His protective embrace always keep you and your loved ones enveloped in the warmth of constant joy.

May I now draw your attention to these points please:

1. A beautiful flower is one of the truest blessings of God.
2. And that is because such beauty is all selfless: all its fragrance, all its beauty, all its honey - everything is meant for others - it simply keeps nothing for itself!
3. That is the ultimate essence of beauty, giving flowers the highest eligibility to constitute the holiest offering to God.

Wishing you joy as ever,
With love and blessings,
Debanjan

3. Rejoice in the Dulcet Beauty of a Glorious Sunset

Dear Brothers and Sisters,

Prayers to God for your brilliant success in life. May His protective embrace always keep you and your loved ones enveloped in the warmth of constant joy.

May I now draw your attention to these points please:

1. The serene beauty of a sunset is a sublime blessing of God.
2. Then, the red orb of the sun starts slow descent into the horizon, the sky on the western front begins to display a fascinating range of colours, the birds start flying home and a sense of stillness lends its soothing balm all around.

3. The overall effect is that of an exquisite serenity, that can only be experienced.
4. And given our frenzied lifestyles, such tranquillity is a blessing that can truly rejuvenate us.
5. So, let us take out just a few minutes of our daily grind to step out at the time of sunset and rejoice in its dulcet beauty.

Wishing you joy as ever,
With love and blessings,
Debanjan

FOUR

The Blessings of Daily Life (Theme: Happiness)

Friends, under this joyful theme, I have included the following blessings:

1. To seek forgiveness is divine
2. To forgive is blissful
3. Companionship of the good = Source of all Good in Life
4. Master-key of virtue unlocks the prison of vice

I am now placing them for your kind reading here:

1. To Seek Forgiveness is Divine

Dear Brothers and Sisters,

Prayers to God for your brilliant success in life. May His protective embrace always keep you and your loved ones enveloped in the warmth of constant joy.

May I now draw your attention to these points please:

1. Seeking forgiveness is truly divine, because our Heavenly Father, God dwells in the heart of each man.
2. Hence, by saying the magical five-letter word SORRY to another man, we basically acknowledge this fundamental truth and thus manifest our inner Divinity.
3. Plus, the very thinking process that inspires us to say SORRY, makes us humble.
4. And, humility, of course, is the essential pillar of character.
5. Let us please ponder on these thoughts and imbibe the crux into our day-to-day living.

Wishing you the soothing bliss of peace of mind,
With love and blessings,
Debanjan

2. To Forgive is Blissful

Dear Brothers and Sisters,

Prayers to God for your brilliant success in life. May His protective embrace always keep you and your loved ones enveloped in the warmth of constant joy.

May I now draw your attention to these points please:

1. Among all acts of Divinity that we can perform voluntarily, forgiving another person fully and freely, comes right at the top.

2. Now that person includes everyone who may have hurt us in the past through words, deeds or otherwise in any manner.
3. But when we CHOOSE to forgive him, we basically CHOOSE to come out of our self-imposed prison of lingering hatred.
4. Thereby, we CHOOSE to come out into the sunshine of peace.
5. And peace is that divine blessing that connects us straight to God.

Wishing you soothing peace of mind in your life,
With love and blessings,
Debanjan

3. The Companionship of Good = Source of all Good in Life

Dear Brothers and Sisters,

Prayers to God for your brilliant success in life. May His protective embrace always keep you and your loved ones enveloped in the warmth of security.

May I now draw your attention to these points please:

1. Good has got tremendous power.
2. And we keep on coming into contact with Good in various forms in our day-to-day life.
3. Good may be in the form of profound sayings of a realized Saint; it can be a passage from our Holy Scriptures containing the words of God; it can be an inspiring biography of a Great man; it can be the daily blessings of Mother Nature and so on.

4. And, when we come into contact with Good, we gradually but inexorably start imbibing those divine virtues in our character.
5. And, Good = God and God = Good.
6. So, by our decision to seek the companionship of the Good, we bring the power of God into our own lives.
7. Hence, let us always cultivate the companionship of the Good.

Wishing you joy as ever,
With love and blessings,
Debanjan

4. The Master-key of Virtue = Freedom from the Prison of Vice

Dear Brothers and Sisters,

Prayers to God for your brilliant success in life. May His protective embrace always keep you and your loved ones enveloped in the warmth of constant joy.

May I now draw your attention to these points please:

1. In this post we focus on the divine benediction, that accrues to us, when we let the sunshine of virtues illuminate our lives.
2. Its powerfully penetrating rays, then break down the flimsy miasma of vice, that often manages to creep into our character over a period of time.
3. That is a supreme power of virtue that encompasses the whole gamut of divine qualities such as joy, compassion, moral courage, single-minded focus, iron-will and so on.
4. In this context, it will be tremendously profitable, to recall two wonderfully uplifting parables shared by God

Incarnate of our modern age, Sri Ramakrishna Dev:

i. When we bring light into a room shrouded in darkness since long, the redeeming power of light drives away the blackness of the latter in a single instant. Similarly, the torch of virtue banishes the blackness of the vice at once.
ii. When we decide to walk towards a holy town such as Kashi and away from a worldly town such as Kolkata, then each step towards the former (representing virtue), takes us automatically away from the latter (representing vice).

1. How liberating the above concepts are...!!
2. So, let us reflect on such divine inspiration and start walking on the path of virtue from right now onwards.

Wishing you joy as ever,
With love and blessings,
Debanjan

FIVE

THE BLESSINGS OF DAILY LIFE (THEME: GOODNESS)

Friends, under this noble theme, I have included the following blessings:

1. Every Single Day is a Day of Renewal
2. Happiness is Our Own Choice
3. Give with Joy

I am now placing them for your kind reading here:

1. Every Single Day is a Day of Renewal

Dear Brothers and Sisters,

Prayers to God for your brilliant success in life. May His protective embrace always keep you and your loved ones enveloped in the warmth of constant joy.

May I now draw your attention to these points please:

1. As we travel the ups and downs of this ephemeral life, we are often subjected to setbacks and disappointments.
2. But, let us always try to remember that no setback is permanent, provided we keep a strong belief in ourselves.
3. That is because God resides within each one of us and whenever we get lost, He guides us back to the righteous path.
4. So, trusting in God, let us renew our efforts again.
5. A fresh day will arrive tomorrow, sent just for us, by God.

Wishing you joy as ever,
With love and blessings,
Debanjan

2. Happiness is Our Own Choice

Dear Brothers and Sisters,

Prayers to God for your brilliant success in life. May His protective embrace always keep you and your loved ones enveloped in the warmth of constant joy.

May I now draw your attention to these points please:

1. In this post, let us briefly attempt exploring the basic message of the captioned title.
2. We shall then see how the conscious cultivation of this idea can connect us back to God.
3. Now, you may question the very basis of the claim: "happiness is our own choice".

4. You very well argue that in a world, mired in ruthless competition and mindless chasing of money at all cost, how can this ever be possible.
5. You may rightly say competition, through its win-loss outcome, will generate unhappiness as the inevitable by-product.
6. But, a little self-reflection will show that happiness is an output of our own internal process: it is NOT contingent upon external conditions of people and circumstances. Yes, this is true indeed...!
7. And that is because, as the master of our ship, we can exercise our divine power of CHOICE.
8. For instance, we may CONSCIOUSLY decide to keep our mind centred on God, irrespective of what is going on around us.
9. And happiness is the assured outcome of such a DELIBERATELY positive thinking process.
10. In other words, irrespective of past setbacks in our lives, irrespective of less-than-civilized behaviour of others (and the list of negativities may go on...), we can still choose to keep our minds raised upward and fixed upon God. Remember God is the eternal entity of the GOOD in the whole cosmos.
11. When we cultivate such a deliberate God-centred thinking process, the virtue of goodness starts permeating our entire being.
12. And, on this fertile soil of inner purity grows the delicate plant of equanimity, on which blooms the precious flower of HAPPINESS.
13. This process can't be explained employing just words alone - it has to be actually experienced by us in person.
14. Therefore, in the footsteps of brother Lawrence, let us strive to consciously practice the 'Presence of God' in our

lives and reap its divine fruit of happiness thereafter.

Wishing you joy as ever,
With love and blessings,
Debanjan

3. Give with Joy

Dear Brothers and Sisters,

Prayers to God for your brilliant success in life. May His protective embrace always keep you and your loved ones enveloped in the warmth of constant joy.

May I now draw your attention to these points please:

1. As you all know, this human life is transient.
2. We can take nothing from here, when we depart, except for merits we acquire in our lifetimes.
3. And, the best path to earn such merits is giving and sharing what we have with others, freely and joyfully.
4. The bliss of this divine way of living can only be savoured by the actual experience of giving with joy.
5. Hence, I humbly request all of you, to try this philosophy of living and see the outcome for yourself.

Wishing you all happiness.
With love and blessings,
Debanjan

SIX

THE BLESSINGS OF DAILY LIFE (THEME: SUCCESS)

Friends, under this life-transforming theme, I have included the following blessings:

1. Consistency is the Key to Success
2. Be True to Yourself
3. Catch Yourself Doing Right
4. Start Small Always

I am now placing these blessings for your kind reading here:

1. Consistency is the Key to Success

Dear Brothers and Sisters,

Prayers to God for your brilliant success in life. May His protective embrace always keep you and your loved ones enveloped in the warmth of constant joy.

May I now draw your attention to these points please:

1. The very word "CONSISTENCY" conjures up an image of a person, performing the same activity, over and over again. And that is the right image indeed.
2. Consistency is the very foundation on which the pillars of success stand.
3. Now, why should this be so?
4. A little reflection will show us that, if we really want our endeavour to be fruitful, then we need to persist in repeating it day in and day out.
5. An illustration will be helpful here: suppose we want to succeed in writing a new book, then we would need to master the discipline of consistently writing for a set duration of time every day and producing a minimum number of words as output.
6. Similarly, let us say we want to cultivate the virtue of waking up by 5 AM everyday and make it a part of our character. Then, we would need to be disciplined in all our activities throughout the day and go to sleep by 10 PM on a consistent basis, so that we can wake up early as a matter of habit.
7. And if we want to build a good character, cultivating the company of the good on a consistent basis is the right path.
8. The above example illustrates the central idea of what I want to convey: consistency creates a sustained momentum, which then leads to our success.
9. So, my dear brothers and sisters reading this post, I fervently appeal to you to consistently keep on doing good. You will reap its success one day.

Wishing you success as ever,

With love and blessings,
Debanjan

2. Be True to Yourself

Dear Brothers and Sisters,

Prayers to God for your brilliant success in life. May His protective embrace always keep you and your loved ones enveloped in the warmth of constant joy.

May I now draw your attention to these points please:

1. It is so important to remain true to yourself at all times.
2. This is especially true in a world, where relentless pressure is brought upon us, right from our childhood, to relinquish all our individual God- given uniqueness.
3. Instead, we are expected to conform to so-called 'norms' set by significant 'others' - they include parents, teachers, relatives, friends etc.
4. These so-called 'norms' usually cover the most vital areas of our life like choice of our occupation.
5. These are the areas that ought to be best left to the individual's choice. But sadly, societal pressures make us conform to what is expected of us and any deviation is frowned upon.
6. As an inevitable result, many of us are forced to stifle our God-given talents and join the hordes in some socially acceptable profession.
7. The sad result is lifelong mediocrity and hence, misery.
8. So dear brothers and sisters, it is most important to listen to your own heart, where God resides and preserve your individuality at all costs.
9. Let "you be you" - true happiness lies there only.

Wishing you success as ever,
With love and blessings,
Debanjan

3. Catch Yourself Doing Right

Dear Brothers and Sisters,

Prayers to God for your brilliant success in life. May His protective embrace always keep you and your loved ones enveloped in the warmth of constant joy.

May I now draw your attention to these points please:

1. "Catching ourselves doing right" is the sure-shot 'mantra' of a joyous way of living.
2. Now, this philosophy of success goes directly against our social conditioning all through our lives.
3. For example, we are always taught to 'catch ourselves doing wrong', ostensibly to improve our weaknesses.
4. But that conditioning produces nothing but misery as then, all our time and energy gets focused on 'what we lack'.
5. In sharp contrast, when we condition ourselves to stay alert at all times and catch ourselves doing something right (irrespective of how small that accomplishment may be), then it instantly produces a tiny ripple of joy in our minds.
6. And if we meet each day of our life with this changed mentality, then we start becoming aware of the umpteen things we do right throughout the day. Earlier we might have taken them for granted.
7. This motivates us to accomplish even more things right the next day. This inevitably produces feelings of authentic happiness.

8. The net result is a continuous stream of joy animating our life each day.

Wishing you success as ever,
With love and blessings,
Debanjan

4. Start Small Always

Dear Brothers and Sisters,

Prayers to God for your brilliant success in life. May His protective embrace always keep you and your loved ones enveloped in the warmth of constant happiness.

May I now draw your attention to these points please:

1. Let us always remember that God has given each of us a specific mission in life.
2. So, it is of paramount importance to relentlessly strive towards its accomplishment.
3. We gradually get to know about this mission when we still ourselves to listen to the voice of God, speaking to us in the silence of our hearts.
4. Once we get an inkling about our mission, then we need to start on that path right away.
5. Now, initially let us start small, so that we can learn and improve as we go along.
6. And if we are sincere enough, we shall start achieving small wins - that will induce the extremely powerful mechanisms of the virtuous cycle to come into force.
7. That will propel us towards even bigger wins on the path to achieve our mission.
8. And, the direct spin-off from such positive momentum will be a tremendous gain in authentic happiness for us.

Wishing you success as ever,
With love and blessings,
Debanjan

SEVEN

THE BLESSINGS OF DAILY LIFE (THEME: ATTITUDE)

Friends, under this theme of supreme importance, I have included the following blessings:

1. The Greatest Human Freedom = The Freedom to Choose
2. Bless Those Who Hurt You
3. Right Thinking Leads to Right Action
4. See Poetry in the Common-place Events of Daily Life

I am now placing these blessings for your kind reading here:

1. The Greatest Human Freedom =The Freedom to Choose

Dear Brothers and Sisters,

Prayers to God for your brilliant success in life. May His protective embrace always keep you and your loved ones enveloped in the warmth of constant joy.

May I now draw your attention to these points please:

1. The greatest freedom lies inherent in our power to choose our own desired response in any given situation.
2. All of us, in our day to day lives, routinely encounter situations of discord: the most typical situation is the one where we are dealing with another person and he says/does something unpleasant.
3. In the normal course, we react in a tit for tat, impulsive manner and soon an ugly altercation may ensue - no one wins really.
4. But if we analyse the above situation in a cool-headed manner later, we'll be astounded to discover a stark fact! And the fact is, we had been made into a slave by that other person, for the entire duration of our corrosive interaction!
5. This is because the opposite party has called all the shots by saying or doing something foul and we have nearly responded like a puppet on a string: we have just danced to his tune.
6. But now imagine the same situation, where irrespective of whatever the other party me say/do, <u>we choose to remain unperturbed.</u>
7. And, from that unflappable place of equanimity, it is we who take the lead by choosing our measured response in the face of provocations. Then how liberating it would be...!
8. The opponent would then lose all his power to call the shots and we would regain our power by the same

margin.

9. In other words, irrespective of whatever life may throw at us - we can always choose to remain calm. Oof!! The very thought itself is so empowering...!!
10. Such royal freedom of choice would allow us to navigate the treacherous twist and turns of our unpredictable lives with the divine grace of calmness.
11. Then, our lives would turn into Divine mansions of harmony and peace supreme.

Please reflect on the above line of thought.
With love and blessings,
Debanjan

2. Bless Those Who Hurt You

Dear Brothers and Sisters,

Prayers to God for your brilliant success in life. May His protective embrace always keep you and your loved ones enveloped in the warmth of constant joy.

May I draw your kind attention to the following points please:

1. Now, on the face of it, the title of this letter may appear to be a contradiction in terms. One may logically ask, "How can I bless a person who is hurting me?" Yes, it may appear to be a puzzle at the first glance.
2. Yet, our scriptures teach us this very lesson – so, deep self-reflection will be helpful here. Because, when we cultivate the spiritually enriching practice of looking inwards, we get the sacred touch of God dwelling in our own hearts – then, all our queries get answered by Him.

3. Then, we shall come to realize that when a person abuses us, he's doing us much greater good instead of harm. The following points will explain how.
4. First, when we praise another person's virtue, we're basically drawing in that virtue to our own self. By the same token, when we criticise another person's vice, we attract that very fault into our own character as well. This basically implies the happy conclusion that, when anyone verbally hurts us, we should rejoice as our own character will get a cleansing in this process.
5. Second, when we are getting verbally hurt by another person, it gives us a golden opportunity to bless him with all the divine benedictions - sustained joy, prosperity, good health, abundance, peace, and fulfilment of dreams. And when we bless others, we are ultimately blessing ourselves only for we are all part of the same Divinity.
6. Third and the most important reason is this: God has sent each one of us to this mortal plane with a specific Mission and after accomplishing it, we all return to Him, So, then, during our all too brief mortal journey, we need to keep ourselves religiously focused on that Mission alone - whatever any other mortal being may say or do against us is of absolutely zero consequence here.
7. Fourth, during our temporary stay on this mortal plane, each one of us is under the "Law of Karma": at the end of our limited time on this earth, we all shall be answerable for our actions before God. Remembering this, let us always try to do good to a person abusing us - each one of us will atone for our own action.
8. Fifth, let us also remember that under the supreme "Law of Karma", we are suffering trials now, as punishment for our own actions in the past. Knowing this, let us

learn to calmly accept the supposedly insulting words of others - by doing so, our own previous "Karma" gets expiated.

My dear brothers and sisters, I request each one of you to introspect upon the above message.

Let such self-contemplation illuminate your mind so that you gradually start becoming aware of its truth, by your own self.

With love and blessings,

Debanjan

3. Right Thinking Leads to Right Action

Dear Brothers and Sisters,

Prayers to God for your brilliant success in life. May His protective embrace always keep you and your loved ones enveloped in the warmth of constant joy.

May I now draw your attention to these points please:

1. Let us begin by reflecting on the word "right": we will then come to realise the true significance of this concept.
2. "Right" is that, which is in accordance with God-given principles of honesty, purity, compassion and all other Divine virtues. Hence "right" is a profound ideal indeed.
3. Thus, "right" may look like a small five-letter word, but its extraordinarily wide canvas covers everything a man ever does.
4. Hence, if our internal thought processes are in accordance with God's will, then its external manifestation that is, "action" will follow the same Divine principle also. Because, if the means are right, then the ends are bound to be right all as well.

5. An example from our day-to-day life will be helpful here - when we begin to have the compassionate thought of helping the needy, then it will most probably get translated into the virtuous action of our making a suitable contribution, to a noble institution of charity.
6. And our right thinking, leading to the right action, has to end in the right outcome. Later, that outcome will generate the right thoughts again - that is the biggest plus point of this virtuous cycle.

Request each one of you to contemplate the eternal truth stated above.

Wishing you joy as ever,
With love and blessings,
Debanjan

4. See Poetry in the Common-place Events of Daily Life

Dear Brothers and Sisters,

Prayers to God for your brilliant success in life. May His protective embrace always keep you and your loved ones enveloped in the warmth of constant joy.

May I now draw your attention to these points please:

1. Let's always remember that our happiness lies in our own hands.
2. And, one of the easiest ways to seek happiness is, to slow down our hectic pace of life and take a little pause.
3. That will allow us to see beauty in the commonplace things of our daily life.
4. For example, when we slow down, then we may be able to catch the beautiful colours of the rainbow framed in

oil film left by passing cars on the road. We may then also be able to catch the bubbling sense of joy in the voice of a child playing in the park. And, we may also admire the beautiful patterns, made by sunlight streaming through the leaves of a large tree.

5. All we need is a receptive mind, that makes us alert, to the poetry all around.

Wishing you joy as ever,
With love and blessings,
Debanjan

EIGHT

The Blessings of Daily Life (Theme: Actions and Habits)

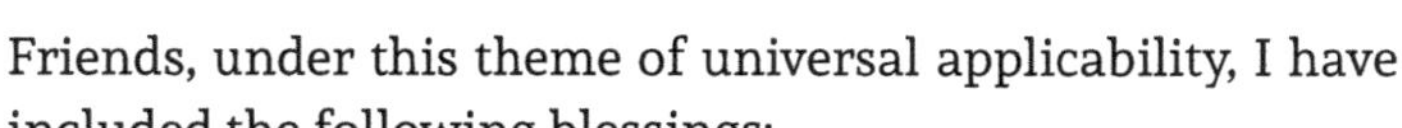

Friends, under this theme of universal applicability, I have included the following blessings:

1. Let Us Think of Others Too...
2. Keeping Promises to Ourselves is Blissful
3. Keep Looking at the Polestar
4. Habit is the Foundation of Life
5. Reflect on Your Day at the end of Each Day

I am now placing these blessings for your kind reading here:

1. Let Us Think of Others Too...

Dear Brothers and Sisters,

Prayers to God for your brilliant success in life. May His protective embrace always keep you and your loved ones enveloped in the warmth of constant joy.

May I now draw your attention to these points please:

1. “Let us think of others too” - initially, this cry may not resonate with us, given the self-centred times we are living in right now.
2. However, when we deeply reflect, then we start gradually realising the wonderful truth present in these few words.
3. The basic reason, why we need to consider one another’s welfare, is the fundamental unity of all of us.
4. In other words, our outer appearance may vary but at the root level, each one of us is an extension of the all-pervading Universal Consciousness: we are all one.
5. Therefore, when we offer our help to another human being apparently distinct from us, we are basically helping ourselves only.
6. There is one additional and equally vital perspective we need to keep in mind: all of us live under the inexorable ‘law of karma’, whereby we reap what we sow - in other words, we get what we give.
7. Thus, when we offer our love and compassion to another living being, in any manner - big or small - that goodness will inevitably return to us sooner or later.

Wishing you joy at all times,
With love and blessings,
Debanjan

2. Keeping Promises to Ourselves is Blissful

Dear Brothers and Sisters,

Prayers to God for your brilliant success in life. May His protective embrace always keep you and your loved ones enveloped in the warmth of constant joy.

May I now draw your attention to these points please:

1. Normally, when we think of keeping promises, we usually take into account pledges made by us to others.
2. But even more important is keeping promises, made by us, to own self. It can include meeting both short term promises (for example, fulfilling an item on our daily to-do list) as well as long term promises (for example, keeping our new year resolution) to ourselves.
3. This is more important because when we fulfil our promises to ourselves, we basically honour God living in our hearts.
4. And, when we do so, then the magic starts happening: - each fulfilled promise starts acting as a tiny brick
5. Soon, a series of such individual bricks starts building up into a wonderful edifice of strong character, resting on the solid foundation of scrupulous integrity and high self-esteem.
6. Undoubtedly, the character is our single biggest asset, in this earthly life.

Wishing you joy as ever,
With love and blessings,
Debanjan

3. Keep Looking at the Polestar

Prayers to God for your brilliant success in life. May His protective embrace always keep you and your loved ones enveloped in the warmth of constant joy.

May I now draw your attention to these points please:

1. In scriptures, the continual ups and downs of our earthly lives have been compared to the relentless rise and fall of ocean waves.
2. Since life is so turbulent, it is of utmost importance to fix our sight on the constant landmark of the 'polestar' so that we can navigate our way forward in life.
3. <u>And, that polestar is God, who is eternal and unchanging.</u>
4. Thus, let us always keep our minds attuned to God through constant prayers.
5. And, let us seek His Grace at every moment so that we can cross this ocean of life safely.

Wishing you joy as ever,
With love and blessings,
Debanjan

<u>4. Habit is the Foundation of Life</u>

Dear Brothers and Sisters,

Prayers to God for your brilliant success in life. May His protective embrace always keep you and your loved ones enveloped in the warmth of constant joy.

May I now draw your attention to these points please:

1. As we reflect on the apparently simple but extremely powerful five-letter word H...A...B...I...T, we shall gradually realise that this one single constituent of our

daily life will more or less determine a stark outcome.

2. And that outcome would be, at the end of our transient life, whether we'll pass away in contentment or we'll depart amidst futile regret.
3. If we've taken care to cultivate good habits, then we'll be propelled inexorably along the path of utilizing our limited time on this mortal plane, towards accomplishing the God-given Mission of our life.
4. But if we happen to pick up a bad habit, then we'll end up recklessly squandering away that little bit of time with sad but imaginable results.
5. Example of a good habit would be, a daily custom of writing the three most important goals for the next day, before going to bed.
6. This will put in motion, the divine blessings of the virtuous cycle: the more wins we score by achieving our daily goals, the more will our authentic self-worth grow, which in turn will encourage us to set bigger goals and achieve even more.
7. The end result would be a wonderfully productive life, infused with the true joy of authentic accomplishments.
8. Therefore, my dear brothers and sisters, let us introspect on the extraordinary powers of our daily HABITS to either make or mar our lives.
9. Which habit shall we cultivate? The choice is ours.

Wishing you joy at all times,
With love and blessings,
Debanjan

5. Reflect on Your Day at the end of Each Day

Dear Brothers and Sisters,

Prayers to God for your brilliant success in life. May His protective embrace always keep you and your loved ones enveloped in the warmth of constant joy.

May I now draw your attention to these points please:

1. Time is flowing away at each instant with tremendous speed; however, most of us lead a life, oblivious to this plain fact.
2. One effective way of countering this widely prevalent tendency, is, to sit down at the end of each day, be still and quietly reflect on the day that has just gone by.
3. In each such session, let us ask ourselves, "Today, have I moved in the direction in which I want my life to move?"
4. Asking this question to ourselves, though often uncomfortable, will force us to come face-to-face with how we have chosen to spend the day:

i. have we shown full respect to the day through wise investment of time?

Or,

i. have we shown disrespect by just squandering the day away?

5. And, then based on our learning from such self-introspection, we can begin moulding the days to follow in the desired direction.
6. So, let's decide wisely: each day is God's best gift to us.

Wishing you joy as ever,
With love and blessings,
Debanjan

NINE

The Blessings of Daily Life (Theme: Learning)

Friends, under this theme of great significance, I have included the following blessings:

1. A Good Book > A King's Treasury
2. Education is That Which Builds our Character
3. Biographies of Great Men are Tremendously Inspirational
4. Education is Manifestation of Perfection Inherent in Man

I am now placing these blessings for your kind reading here:

1. A Good Book is More Precious than a King's Treasury

Dear Brothers and Sisters,

Prayers to God for your brilliant success in life. May His protective embrace always keep you and your loved ones enveloped in the warmth of constant joy.

May I now draw your attention to these points please:

1. It is a beautiful fact of life that a good book is more valuable than all the gold in possession of a King.
2. That is because, the knowledge we gain through a good book is never lost, while the material treasures of this ephemeral life are inevitably subject to decay and loss, over time.
3. Therefore, when we deliberately choose to read a good book, we start changing for the better inside us.
4. Basically, deep inside us, our thinking gets more and more purified and in life, a pure thought process is the root cause of all joy.
5. Hence, in a nutshell, a good book is the fountainhead of joy.
6. That is why a good book will always be more precious than all the material riches of a King.

Wishing you joy as ever,
With love and blessings,
Debanjan

2. Education is That Which Builds our Character

Dear Brothers and Sisters,

Prayers to God for your brilliant success in life. May His protective embrace always keep you and your loved ones enveloped in the warmth of constant joy.

May I now draw your attention to these points please:

1. Education, in its true essence, raises us from animality to humanity and thence, from humanity to divinity.
2. It is this process of elevation, which results in the manifestation of virtues, already present within us in latent form.
3. Therefore, the outcome of true education is a virtuous man.
4. And, the presence of virtues is the very epitome of a sound character.
5. Hence, education is that, which builds our Character.

Wishing you joy as ever,
With love and blessings,
Debanjan

3. Biographies of Great Men are Tremendously Inspirational

Dear Brothers and Sisters,

Prayers to God for your brilliant success in life. May His protective embrace always keep you and your loved ones enveloped in the warmth of constant joy.

May I now draw your attention to these points please:

1. Reading biographies of great men is tremendously inspirational.
2. To know why, we may profitably quote from Samuel Smile's great book 'Self-help': "The valuable examples

which they furnish of the power of ... resolute working and steadfast integrity eloquently illustrate the efficacy of ... self-reliance in enabling men of even humblest rank to work out for themselves an honourable competency..."

3. The above points amply make it clear why the reading of biographies constitutes such a powerful means of moulding one's character.
4. So, let us cultivate this golden habit of reading biographies – a good example would be the biography of Benjamin Franklin.
5. Such a habit will definitely lead to amazing results later...!

Wishing you all success,
With love and blessings,
Debanjan

4. Education is Manifestation of Perfection Inherent in Man

Dear Brothers and Sisters,

Prayers to God for your brilliant success in life. May His protective embrace always keep you and your loved ones enveloped in the warmth of constant joy.

May I now draw your attention to these points please:

1. The resounding utterance of Swami Vivekananda, the Sage of modern times, is the captioned title of this post.
2. Let us reflect on the profound insight of this statement and thus purify ourselves.
3. When we begin to reflect on this saying of Swamiji, the prophet of our modern age, our first reaction maybe of surprise.

4. This is because the conventional definition of education signifies teacher pouring in an external stream of knowledge on diverse subjects into his supposedly uneducated student,
5. But deeper introspection reveals to us the profound truth that each one of us is a part and parcel of the Divine Consciousness.
6. That is why the holy Bible says the Kingdom of God is present within
7. Then we our inherently divine nature will imply that we already have everything present within us in dormant form - it just needs a suitable spark, provided by the right teacher, to gradually manifest that repository of knowledge from within us.
8. Stated in another way, the external knowledge being imported by the teacher is like a vibrating tuning fork, that brings about a congruent resonance within the mind of a student.
9. As result, the relevant knowledge already present in a seed form within a student, starts flowering in slow and steady manner - it is in this manner that we get educated in the real sense.
10. In like manner, all divine virtues truth, purity, honesty, fairness and all other forces of good are already present within us.
11. So, even if we happen to stray into the wrong path under the incessant pressures of this corrupted age, nothing is lost.
12. All we need to do, is to remember our innate divine nature and come back to the path of God.
13. How reassuring this line of thought is...!!

So, come, let each one of us meditate on this uplifting wisdom and mould our lives accordingly.

With love and blessings,

Debanjan

TEN

AN EARNEST HOPE

Friends, hope these letters have given something for you to think about. And, as I have realized while writing these letters, it is our thinking which is at the root cause of everything in life.

The right kind of thinking always leads to happiness, success, and fulfilment. And in an exactly similar way, the wrong thinking leads to the unwelcome opposite. So, therefore, if reading these letters makes you embark on your own journey of self-contemplation and thus, slowly makes you a higher thinker, then the purpose of this book will have been served.

With these words, I bid you adieu and hope your journey in life is ever filled with adventure and discovery.

May God bless all with joy and abundance.

Thank you.

9 798886 843934